# Financial Flow
## *Mindful Wealth Management for Prosperity*

# Table of Contents

# Chapter 1. Introduction

In the enchanting world of finance, the dance between money and mindfulness often seems like a distant dream. Our Special Report, "Financial Flow: Mindful Wealth Management for Prosperity" seeks to blend these two apparently divergent realms into a harmonious symphony. Unmask the secrets of sustainable wealth creation and nourish your prosperity garden with the nurturing essence of mindfulness. Beware, this is not a story of overnight riches, but an enlightening journey to financial peace. This report, enriched with insights from industry stalwarts and buoyed by practical, easy-to-adapt strategies, promises an engaging exploration of mindful wealth management. So, buckle up, dear reader. Turn this page and embark on this enticing roller-coaster of finance – where terms 'wealth' and 'happiness' comfortably coexist. Don't just read – savor it, breath it, live it. This Special Report isn't just another financial guide; it's your path toward a prosperous life brimming with financial serenity!

# Chapter 2. Laying the Foundation: Understanding Your Financial Self

To truly manage wealth and assets with mindfulness, there has to be a foundation that defines monetary success, not by the numbers alone but also through our understandings, principles, and decisions. Deciphering what financial prosperity means to you enables you to gauge, mold, and navigate the road to holistic wealth. Understanding your financial self lies at the heart of this journey.

## 2.1. Truth about Your Relationship with Money

Understanding your financial identity involves examining your relationship with money. Money is often a tool that brings choices, freedom, security, and sometimes anxiety. Your emotional state when managing finances provides clues about your behaviors and beliefs. Perhaps saving money gives you a sense of security, or investing might trigger anxiety. Some might see wealth as a symbol of success, while others may equate it with greed. Unearth your notions and prejudices about money to establish your unique financial identity.

## 2.2. Financial Memories and Their Influence

Every perception is usually formed from past experiences and teachings. Recalling childhood memories about money can offer insight into fears, aspirations, and values connected to it. Consider occurrences when money sparked conflict, the financial philosophies of your parents, lessons taught to you about money, and recollect your sentiments associated with these memories. Even minor incidents can have a significant impact on your financial behavior today.

## 2.3. Financial Goals: Long, Medium, and Short-term

We tend to overlook the importance of visualizing our finances in the longer term. Segregating your financial goals into long, medium, and short-term categories gives clarity and purpose to your wealth management journey. Long-term goals might include retirement plans or property purchase, medium-term ones can center around children's education or a dream vacation, while short-term goals might encompass an emergency fund or tax-saving investments.

## 2.4. Financial Status Check

A realistic assessment of your current financial status is imperative. Create a personal balance sheet and calculate your net worth by subtracting liabilities from assets. Record your income and expenses to understand your cash flow. This is not to intimidate or overwhelm you but encourages honesty with your monetary situation. Analyze which areas require improvement and plan remedial actions.

## 2.5. Your Risk Appetite and Investment Psychology

Testing your risk tolerance level helps you make informed financial decisions. Are you willing to dive into ventures that promise high returns but carry significant risks? Or, do you prefer safe investments, even if they yield lower returns? Recognizing your 'risk appetite' influences your investment strategies.

## 2.6. Understanding Interest Rates and Inflation

An understanding of interest rates and inflation is central to financial literacy. Changes in interest rates impact savings and investments. Similarly, inflation decreases the purchasing power of money. Understanding these macroeconomic factors can aid you in making adjustments to your financial planning when needed.

## 2.7. Demystifying Financial Jargon

Grasping financial terminology can seem daunting, but it's a crucial part of understanding your financial self. Terms such as asset, liability, equity, stocks and bonds, mutual funds, diversification, portfolio, capital, liquidity, and others are fundamental concepts that you must understand.

## 2.8. Your Relationship Towards Debt

Debt isn't always a bad thing, but your attitude towards it can shape your financial health significantly. Whether it's credit card debt, student loans, mortgages, or personal loans, identify your perspective towards these financial obligations and assess if your current debt management strategy is sustainable or requires modification.

## 2.9. Estate Planning and Contingency Plans

Estate planning isn't solely for the wealthy. Having contingency plans and ensuring that your loved ones are cared for financially is crucial. This could encompass creating wills, assigning power of attorneys, setting up trusts, obtaining life insurance, and arranging for efficient wealth transfer.

## 2.10. Importance of Financial Education

Taking a proactive approach to learn about money management is a building block for financial stability. To stay informed, read books, join financial wellness seminars, listen to finance podcasts, or leverage online resources. Being financially literate liberates you from the anxiety and uncertainty of not knowing and empowers you to actively engage in financial planning.

With a clear understanding of these facts about your financial position, feelings, memories, and tolerance for risk, you create a sturdy foundation upon which mindful wealth management can grow. The rest of your journey to financial peace will be a steady climb built upon this foundation, leading you to the prosperous life that you envisage.

# Chapter 3. Mindfulness: Unlocking Financial Consciousness

To truly engage with mindful wealth management, we must first endeavor to unlock the realm of financial consciousness. In this chapter, we will delve into the heart of mindfulness and illustrate how it bridges the gap to our financial consciousness, a crucial step in obtaining sustainable prosperity.

## 3.1. The Consciousness-Mindfulness Connection

Consciousness is our inherent awareness or perception of something within ourselves or our environment. Financial consciousness, then, refers to having a keen awareness of our finances: where our money is going, how it's being used, and whether it is effectively contributing to our objectives. However, to attain a high degree of financial consciousness, one must first cultivate mindfulness.

Mindfulness, in its simplest explanation, refers to being in the present moment- completely aware and engaged with whatever activity we are doing or feelings we are experiencing. It is about recognizing our thoughts, emotions, and actions without judgment. From checking emotions at the stock market roller-coaster, to making well-thought-out investment decisions, to gaining satisfaction from saving, mindfulness could be the key to unlocking the door to financial consciousness.

## 3.2. Cultivating Mindfulness

Mindfulness isn't something that manifests overnight. It's a skill to be nurtured and cultivated, honed and applied. And here are ways you can embark on this rewarding journey.

1. Be in the Present Moment: We dwell in past regrets or future uncertainties when it comes to finances. Set that aside for a moment. Not to ignore or forget, but to focus on being in the now. What are you spending on this moment, and why? Being completely present can offer clarity like never before.

2. Acknowledge Emotions Without Judgment: Feelings of stress, worry and even excitement about finances are natural, given money's intertwined relation with our life. However, acknowledging these emotions without judging yourself brings in calmness and objectivity.

3. Practice Gratitude: Align your financial decision making process with the practice of gratitude. Make note of how you are able to sustain your life because of what you have and this can make you take more informed decisions about spending, saving and investing.

## 3.3. The Art of Mindful Spending

Having honed mindfulness, you can now bring it into action: mindful spending. Here, you examine each financial decision - no matter how trivial - under the lens of awareness.

Before making a purchase, ask: . What emotions am I experiencing? . Do I need this or want this? . Will it offer me long-term joy?

Answering them truthfully can keep impulsive buying at bay, leading to fewer regrets and increased satisfaction. Remember, wealth is not merely about accumulation — it's also about the peace derived from mindful, considered choices.

## 3.4. Building a Mindful Budget

Building a mindful budget is an extension of mindful spending. It involves keeping track of your income and expenses, but more than that, it inculcates the essence of being in the moment with every financial decision.

In creating a mindful budget, consider: . Your Values: Align your budget to what truly matters to you. It lends a sense of fulfillment, making the process of sticking to a budget, less of a chore and more of a contentment-inducing practice.

1. Awareness of Income and Expenditure: Be completely aware of your income and how much you're spending. This necessitates regular reviews and updates of your budget.

2. Consider the Future: While being in the present is key, mindful budgeting also involves being conscious of the future. Keep in mind your larger, long-term financial goals. Remember, the idea is to balance contentment today with security for tomorrow.

## 3.5. Mindful Investing

Much as with spending and budgeting, the principles of mindfulness can be applied to investing. This implies remaining composed amidst the stock market's ebbs and flows, and making mindful decisions based on thorough research and personal financial goals.

Mindful investing involves: . Setting Clear Objectives: Clarity about why you're investing boosts your commitment, making you less likely to make hasty, impulsive decisions.

1. Diversification: Diversified investments are a sign of a mindful investor - one who acknowledges that each investment comes with its own set of risks and rewards, and balances them to build a robust portfolio.

2. Regular Review: The mindful investor doesn't 'set and forget'. They track progress, stay updated, and are prepared to adjust their investments as per market dynamics and personal financial situations.

## 3.6. Path to Financially Conscious Decisions

As you journey through the practice of mindfulness, you begin to unlock the realm of financial consciousness. You start being more mindful about your spending, your saving, and more importantly, how you view your money.

Through consistent, aware decision-making, you begin to build wealth mindfully - prioritizing your well-being and financial peace. The path to financial consciousness can appear demanding and exhausting, but with mindfulness at its core, it becomes liberating and enlightening, offering not just the prospect of prosperity, but the reality of financial serenity.

As you make your wealthy path ahead, remember, it's not merely about monetary growth, but a wholesome blend of prosperity and peace of mind. It's about making wealth and happiness comfortable roommates in the grand house of life. And this, dear reader, is the enchanting dance of money and mindfulness.

# Chapter 4. Creating Solidarity: Debunking Debt Dilemmas

Ever since money made its entrance into human society, debt has followed close at heel. Witnessed in ancient civilizations, feudal societies, and modern economies alike, it has shaped and influenced the course of humanity. Thus, debunking debt dilemmas, and understanding it in a more profound and pragmatic way leads to the creation of financial and personal solidarity.

## 4.1. Understanding Debt In Modern Economic Standpoint

We operate in an economy where debt is not only widespread but, often, essential. Debt undergirds homes bought, businesses initiated, education pursued, and dreams realized. This is not to over-glamorize the role of debt in our lives, but rather, to contextualize it. In our pursuit of economic sustainability, we must recognize that debt, balanced by mindfulness and well-managed, can be a useful tool.

Debt becomes our foe when it spirals out of control, draining savings, straining relationships, and stressing mental health. Understanding the nature of debt, learning when it's necessary, and gauging how to manage it are crucial steps toward mindful wealth management.

## 4.2. Debt Management: Working With Interest Rates

One of the key aspects of debt management rests with understanding and working with interest rates. In theory, higher interest rates encourage savings and discourage borrowing, while lower interest rates can stimulate borrowing and spending. Sounds rather straightforward, right? Unfortunately, situations in life are rarely as simple as they seem.

Getting the best out of interest rates requires insight into credit scores, market trends, and the ability to discern between the types of debt. Awareness of the current state of your debt, its impact on credit scores and future borrowing ability, and the fluctuating nature of interest rates are necessary for effective debt management, leading to the cultivation of your prosperity garden.

# 4.3. Unmasking The Good and Bad Debt Theory

The concept distinguishing 'good' and 'bad' debt is deeply rooted in the understanding and use of borrowed money. Good debt is generally considered an investment that will grow in value or generate long-term income. Taking out student loans to pay for a college education, or borrowing to buy a home or car are classically considered examples of good debt.

On the contrary, bad debt refers to borrowing money for short-term desires or consumables that do not generate any long-term benefits. Credit card debt often falls into this category, especially if it's being used to cover daily expenses that extend beyond your income. Unmasking the distinction between good and bad debt enables you to re-evaluate your borrowing habits, and pivot towards a more mindful approach.

## 4.4. The Debt Snowball Method: Tangible Steps to Freedom

Originated by personal finance expert Dave Ramsey, the Debt Snowball Method is a strategy for eliminating personal debt. You begin by targeting the smallest debt first, while maintaining minimum payments on all other obligations, thus gaining momentum as each debt is paid off. This strategy is not only a practical approach to managing debt but can yield a considerable psychological boost as your indebtedness visibly decreases.

## 4.5. The Debt Avalanche Method: Another Route to Liberation

Alternatively, the Debt Avalanche Method advocates for paying off the debt with the highest interest rate first. Though this method can save more money over time in interest payments, it often requires more time to see the initial results, which can be discouraging for some individuals.

Selecting the right method to manage debt depends greatly on your individual financial situation and your psychological propensity towards debt. Both strategies gear towards the ultimate goal: financial freedom.

This chapter is not an exhaustive guide to overcoming debt but serves as a catalyst for reframing your perspective on borrowing, spending, and saving. In the enchanting world of finance, where money and mindfulness dance in harmony, resolving debt dilemmas is a significant step towards cultivating a prosperous life. Developing a deep, mindful understanding of debt decodes one of the critical elements of wealth management.

This journey calls for vigilance, mindfulness, prudence, and resilience: it is not for the faint-hearted but lends a richer texture to our journey toward a mindful, prosperous life. Combining fiscal acumen with personal resilience, let's assist each other in establishing financial solidarity. Debunking debt dilemmas: one mindful step at a time.

# Chapter 5. Savings Sanctuary: Fostering a Culture of Savings

Creating an environment that encourages savings is a critical step towards achieving financial peace and prosperity. The process, though instrumental in the formation of long-term wealth, often gets overlooked amidst the frantic pursuit of immediate gratification. This segment invites you to step into a sanctuary of savings and acquaints you with its essential elements.

## 5.1. The Philosophy of Savings

Understanding the philosophy of savings is key to ingraining this practice into your lifestyle. It's not just about setting aside a portion of your income each month. Rather, it's a fundamental mindset that influences your perception of money and guides your expenditure habits. A saver's mindset revolves around prioritizing long-term goals, appreciating the power of delay, and valuing the virtue of satisfying needs over wants. If money is the seed of wealth, then savings is the soil in which it grows.

## 5.2. The Concept of Paying Yourself First

A crucial technique to foster a culture of savings is to "Pay Yourself First." Rather than depositing only what's left after expenses into your savings, the idea is to immediately set aside a predetermined percentage of your income for savings as soon as you receive it. This philosophy rightly places saving on the pedestal of fiscal priorities – before bills, before discretionary spending, before any and all financial obligations.

## 5.3. Organizing Your Personal Finances

Organizing your personal finances can seem like an uphill battle at first, but it's a task that bears fruitful returns. Start by understanding your present financial situation – your income, expenses, debts, and savings. Analyze every aspect minutely. Always aim for a positive cash flow, which signifies that you're earning more than you're spending. Use budgets as financial compasses to guide your spending decisions while giving due attention to savings.

## 5.4. Emergency Funds: The First Battle Station

An emergency fund serves as your first line of defense against unforeseen expenditures. It should contain enough money to cover about three to six months' worth of living expenses. Not only does it act as a safety net, but it also provides mental comfort. Once this is in place, you can confidently navigate through financial emergencies without raiding your long-term savings.

## 5.5. Understanding and Using Various Savings Products

Savings isn't a one-size-fits-all endeavor; there are various financial vehicles available that can help grow your wealth. Bank savings accounts, money market funds, Certificates of Deposits, and bonds are but some of these. Each has its own benefits and is suited to different saving objectives. A comprehensive understanding of available options will enable you to craft a savings strategy that aligns with your financial goals.

## 5.6. New Age Savings: Exploiting Technology

The revolution of FinTech has democratized access to financial services and has made saving easier than ever before. Apps and platforms provide automated savings options, round-up investment features, and real-time expense tracking. Such digitized finance aids can augment a culture of savings and are especially useful to those embarking on their savings journey.

## 5.7. Debt Repayment: The Stealthy Savings

Repaying debt often isn't viewed as a saving behavior. However, by paying off debts early, you save on the accumulated interest charges. This is a stealthy form of saving. By reducing or completely eliminating high-interest debts, you're not just creating a positive cash flow but also paving a path towards accelerated savings.

## 5.8. The Art of Conscious Consumption

A culture of savings doesn't necessitate austere living. It encourages, instead, conscious consumption – making thoughtful purchasing decisions to avoid wasteful spending. This art of mindful spending balances the joy of present consumption with the assurance of future financial security.

# 5.9. Inflation: The Silent Erosion

Inflation is the quiet destroyer of purchasing power. It's essential to understand its impact on your savings. If the growth rate of your savings falls behind the rate of inflation, your money slowly but surely loses its value. Including inflation-proofing measures in your savings plan is a must to truly safeguard and grow your wealth.

By engraining these practices in your everyday life, you can foster a culture of savings, a sanctuary where sustainable wealth creation thrives. Remember that the journey to financial peace begins with a single step, taken consistently over time. It's about the process, not just the end result. Offer patience and perseverance – the pillars of mindful wealth creation – and allow them to guide you toward financial serenity.

# Chapter 6. Investment Illumination: Mindful Portfolios

First, we need to acknowledge the inherent paradox in investment: seek returns, yet also safeguard wealth. This dichotomy often trips up even seasoned investors. Mindful investing helps transcend this paradox by merging the pecuniary with the tranquil. Let's dissect this concept further to reinforce your investment understanding and efficacy.

## 6.1. The Concept of Mindful Investing

Imagine a mariner navigating turbulent seas. His success hinges not just on a compass and map, but also his alertness to changes in the environment and his calmness in confronting the unknown. Much like investing, the critical element isn't just knowledge – it's also awareness.

Mindful investment begins with self-awareness and an open mind. Acceptance of market realities, recognition of financial goals, and acknowledgement of personal biases are key. It's forging a unique financial strategy that isn't swayed easily by market tides or parroting successful investors, but rooted in self-understanding, market consciousness, and thoughtfulness.

## 6.2. Building Your Mindful Portfolio

Building a mindful portfolio necessitates understanding the risk spectrums and balancing them with your goals, values, and emotional thresholds. This quintessentially means constructing a personalized investment strategy. Here, we decode this process:

*Table 1. Portfolio Construction – An Overview*

| 1 | Identify Your Financial Goals | Short-term expenses or long-term retirement plan? |
|---|---|---|
| 2 | Recognize Your Risk Tolerance | Capacity to withstand market volatility. |
| 3 | Diversify Investments | Spread risk across asset classes – bonds, equities, commodities. |
| 4 | Review and Rebalance | Regularly adjust the portfolio based on performance and changing goals. |

# 6.3. Delving Deeper: Risk and Diversification

Before you dive into investment, comprehending risk is pivotal. Risk can be market-induced (market risk), specific to a business sector (sectoral risk), or related to a specific investment (company risk). By diversifying portfolios, risks can be managed better and yield a smoother investment journey.

Also, remember that diversification isn't just about adding more assets. It's about adding non-correlated assets – ones that don't simultaneously respond similarly to market movements. Only then can losses in one sector be potentially compensated for by gains in another.

## 6.4. The Art of Review and Rebalance

A common fallacy persists that once created, a portfolio is set in stone. However, a mindful portfolio is like a living organism, needing regular check-ups and adjustments.

Review your portfolio semi-annually or annually. Check if your investments align with your financial goals, risk tolerance, and market realities. If not, rebalancing – realigning the portfolio's asset mix – is imperative. Moving assets from better-performing sectors to those less performing ensures investment alignment with the set goals and subdues the possibility of risk amplification.

## 6.5. Embracing Mindfulness in Investing – Beyond Numbers

While figures and analysis bear significance, mindful investing goes beyond. It embraces the holistic aspect too. ESG (Environmental, Social, Governance) investing reflects this, ensuring investments are not just financially sound but also socially responsible.

Mindful investing is equally about staying centered amidst market chaos and not swaying by investment noise. Mindfulness helps combat cognitive biases – overconfidence, herd mentality, loss aversion – that can jeopardize investment decisions. By consciously investing, you rationalize investment decisions, counteract market frenzy, and ensure sustainable wealth creation.

Indeed, mindful investment is a journey – of unearthing self-awareness, cementing your financial goals, understanding risk, and aligning your actions with values. It's the path to financial serenity that fuses wealth creation with peace of mind. Embrace this journey and illuminate your finances with the beacon of mindfulness.

# Chapter 7. Risk and Reward: A Balanced Perspective

As you journey into the intriguing world of financial management, understanding the twin concepts of 'risk' and 'reward' is crucial. This balance, often likened to the careful dance on a tightrope, requires a delicate blend of knowledge, strategy, and should ideally be rooted in mindfulness.

## 7.1. Understanding Risk and Reward

At its root, risk refers to the potential for an investment to not meet its expected return. In other words, risk represents the possibility of losing some or all of the original investment. Conversely, reward refers to the potential gain that can be earned from an investment. Generally speaking, higher risk is usually coupled with higher potential reward - a concept known as the risk/reward trade-off.

There is an intrinsic link between risk and return, and recognizing this relationship is key in making effective financial decisions. The challenge lies in managing this blend without falling into the trap of fear or greed, two emotions that often lead to unwise investment decisions.

## 7.2. Investing Mindfully: A Risk Perspective

Mindful investing involves looking beyond just financial risk. It incorporates an understanding of your personal concern for various types of risk, such as market risk, interest rate risk, inflation risk, and more importantly, emotional risk - the propensity to make irrational investment decisions under emotional duress.

Start by identifying your risk tolerance, or the level of risk you're comfortable with. This self-awareness will provide the basis for sound investment decisions. It involves introspection, being truthful about your financial goals, and acknowledging your emotional response to potential losses.

Risk tolerance differs for each individual; what might keep one investor awake at night might not phase another. This level of honesty, synced with understanding your financial objectives, matches the essence of mindfulness in investing.

## 7.3. Embracing Reward Mindfully

While risk can induce fear or anxiety, reward, on the other hand, carries the danger of inciting greed. Investors lured by the potential of high returns can often overlook the associated risks, leading to significant financial loss.

In the realm of mindful wealth management, acknowledging the thrill of potential gain imbued with a grounded understanding of possible risk is critical. Practices such as diversification and asset allocation serve to maximize potential rewards while simultaneously minimizing associated risks.

## 7.4. The Role of Diversification

Diversification refers to the strategy of spreading investments across various assets or asset classes to reduce exposure to any single investment or risk. While diversification doesn't guarantee against loss, it is the most important component to achieving your long-range financial goals while minimizing risk.

# 7.5. Asset Allocation: Balancing Risk and Reward

Asset allocation is a strategy that involves spreading investment dollars across different asset classes—like stocks, bonds, and cash—to meet financial objectives. It's about dividing your investment portfolio among different asset categories, both for diversification and an acceptable level of risk.

The optimal asset allocation for you depends on specific factors related to your unique circumstances, such as your risk tolerance, investment goals, and time horizon. To grow wealth thoughtfully, it is essential to periodically review and adjust asset allocation based on life changes, such as nearing retirement age or significant changes to income.

# 7.6. Building a Resilient Investment Portfolio

It's essential to keep in mind that even the best-laid plans can and will change due to the shifting winds of the financial markets. Building a resilient portfolio involves being nimble and able to adapt.

One crucial component in mindful wealth management is regular portfolio rebalancing. This practice ensures that the weightings of investments within a portfolio continue to align with the investor's risk tolerance and investment goals. This disciplined practice requires persistence and detachment from short-term market fluctuations, once again promoting the irrefutable connection between finance and mindfulness.

Creating wealth isn't just about chasing profits, but carefully experimenting with the dance between risk and reward. This dance, much like life itself, is creative, dynamic, and involves understanding and managing the risks involved while maintaining an eternal fascination for the potential rewards.

Remember to confront every financial decision not only with the brain but also with the heart intact. With mindfulness as your ever-constant guide, may your wealth garden flourish - a testament to your patience, wisdom, and thoughtful action. Embrace the dance of risk and reward, and may every step lead you closer to financial serenity!

# Chapter 8. Embracing Economics: Understanding Market Dynamics

The world of economics is both lively and intricate, abounding with diverse factors, theories, market forces, and terms that influence the journey of mindful wealth management. To embrace economics – truly, wholly – one must first learn to understand each stitch in the fabric that forms the quilt of market dynamics.

## 8.1. Decoding the Core Concepts

To provide a solid grounding, let's first decode some core concepts – Demand, Supply, and Price Equilibrium. Demand indicates the quantity of a specific product or service consumers are willing to buy at a given price. Supply, on the other hand, is the amount of a specific product or service producers are willing to sell per given price. The interplay of demand and supply then paves the way to price equilibrium – the price at which the quantity demanded and the quantity supplied meet.

It's a dance of numbers – when demand increases with no change in supply, the price surges; when supply intensifies with unchanged demand, the price drops. The beauty of the price equilibrium is the seamless balance it maintains between what the consumers wish to acquire and what the producers desire to provide. When disrupted, a new balance eventually restores, encompassing an ever-changing economic landscape.

## 8.2. Gaining Insights into the Market Structures

Next, we delve into the knowledge of Market Structures - Perfect Competition, Monopolistic Competition, Oligopoly, and Monopoly. Perfect competition is an idealized market structure where several small firms compete against each other. Marginal utility equals marginal cost, and the forces of supply and demand determine the prices. On the other end, in a Monopoly, a single firm dominates the market, oftentimes leading to higher prices and diminished consumer choices.

Monopolistic Competition finds middle ground whereby multiple firms compete with one another, each asserting some market power due to product differentiation. In an Oligopoly, a small number of large firms control the market, leading to a high degree of interdependence among firms.

Understanding these market structures is imperative to grasp a firm's behaviors, consumer choices, price determination, and shape of market dynamics.

## 8.3. The Power of Macroeconomic Factors

Diving deeper, we confront the broad spectrum of macroeconomic factors exerting influence on the markets. These include factors such as inflation, interest rates, GDP growth, national income, unemployment rates, fiscal and monetary policy, and geopolitical events.

Inflation, deemed as the arch-nemesis of purchasing power, can accelerate or decelerate economic growth depending upon its control. Interest rates cast their shadow on every aspect of finance –

from G-sec yields to bank loans to saving rates. A low-interest-rate regime is often preferred by businesses and consumers alike, boosting consumption and investment.

GDP growth and national income serve as economic growth barometers. High employment rates, concurrently, contribute positively to consumer spending and subsequently to economic vitality. Fiscal policies (taxation and government spending) and monetary policies (interest rates and cash supply) work as reins of the economy, steered by the government and central banks respectively.

It's like an artist's palette – disturbances in one color can drastically alter the entire painting. Therefore, mindful wealth management needs one to stay attuned with these macroeconomic ripples, transforming them into wealth-growing opportunities.

# 8.4. Behavioral Economics and Consumer Psychology

Finally, the bridge between economics and psychology – Behavioral Economics – plays a conspicuous role in wealth management. Factors such as cognitive biases, perception, and past experiences deeply color our financial decisions, often contradicting the classical "rational economic man" model. Here, understanding consumer psychology proves pivotal as it uncovers likelihoods of human fallacies. This serves as our compass, guiding us to make more informed, conscious, and robust decisions.

To fully grasp economics indeed means to embrace the wholeness of market dynamics. It's enticingly complex and nuanced, yet undeniably fascinating. The key to navigating these invigorates through these waves lies in 'mindful economics'. With mindfulness anchored in understanding, you not only learn to predict weather the storm but also ride the waves, leading to a prosperous and financially tranquil existence.

In conclusion, mastering market dynamics isn't solely about acquiring wealth; it's about achieving financial peace. And the journey to this serenity starts with embracing economics, understanding its workings, acknowledging the volatility and yet persisting with confidence. It's about not just enduring the roller-coaster ride but also cherishing it to its fullest.

# Chapter 9. Pension Planning: Securing Your Sunset Years

Preface In life, some things are inevitable; growing older is one of them. This natural progression shouldn't stir fear, but promise a convention of wisdom, modest pace, and deserved relaxation. Unfortunately, many find themselves at the doorsteps of retirement with unanticipated apprehension. Will their finances stretch sufficiently? With an intentional and well-charted course, you can evade such uncertainties. That's the essence of pension planning–securing your peace during the sunset years. But before we dig deeper, let's have an overview of what pension planning is all about.

## 9.1. Understanding Pension Planning

Pension planning is a financial strategy aimed at accumulating a portfolio of assets that will provide you with a steady income during retirement. The process involves making regular savings and investment decisions throughout your active years, considering various market risks and personal circumstances. In essence, a well-executed pension plan ensures that you maintain your desired lifestyle without relying on employment income.

## 9.2. Why Pension Planning is Essential

There are several reasons why pension planning is not just necessary but crucial.

- No one wants to worry about money in their old age. Effective pension planning ensures that you have a regular stream of income, providing a certain level of financial security.

- Healthcare demands surge as one ages. Hence, sufficient savings will shield you from unexpected medical costs without disturbing your everyday expenses.

- It allows you to maintain your independence. With a reliable source of retirement income, the need to rely on family or society diminishes.

# 9.3. Components of a Pension Plan

While the structure and features of a pension plan may vary between countries and plan providers, several elements are generally universal.

1. Contributions: This is the amount you, and possibly your employer, deposit into your pension plan continually.

2. Benefit: This is the income you will receive at retirement. The total benefit is determined by the total contributions made plus the returns on investments made with those contributions.

3. Vesting: This term refers to the ownership of your pension benefits.

4. Investment: The contributions made to your pension are invested to enable the portfolio to grow, offsetting the effect of inflation and swelling the pension pot.

# 9.4. Models of Pension Plans

There are two main models of pension plans: the defined benefit plan and the defined contribution plan.

The Defined Benefit (DB) plan promises a specified monthly benefit at retirement, which is typically a function of the member's salary and years of service. The employer, generally, solely funds these, but some solicit contributions from employees.

On the other hand, the Defined Contribution (DC) plan does not promise a specific amount of benefits at retirement. In these plans, contributions are invested, and the returns on those investments are credited to the individual's account.

# 9.5. Developing Your Pension Plan

A journey of a thousand miles starts with a single step. Here are the steps to creating a pension plan that will secure your sunset years.

1. Establish your retirement needs: Start by estimating your retirement expenditure. This should include living expenses, entertainment, healthcare, helping family members, charity, just to name a few.

2. Evaluate your current situation: Take a clear snapshot of where you are currently. This includes your total savings, investments, liabilities, cash flows, etc.

3. Design your pension strategy: Outline a viable strategy for your pension plan. Decide how much you can save periodically, how often, and where you'll invest the savings.

4. Implement the plan: Take actionable steps to implement your plan. This might involve setting up automatic withdrawals that go straight into your pension fund.

5. Monitoring and adjustment: Regularly review your plan to determine if it's on track or needs adjustments.

# 9.6. Seeking Professional Guidance

Pension planning can be daunting due to its longevity, financial jargon it intertwines, and the mathematical calculations it demands.

That's where retirement and pension planning advisors come into play. These are professionals who can assist in the prudential crafting of your pension blueprint, making sure it aligns with your retirement goals. More than just providing professional advice, they are well-versed in the nitty-gritty of the pension industry. They are akin to financial doctors who diagnose, prescribe, and monitor your financial health.

Remember, planning for your pension is not an eighteen-hour flight; it's a lifelong voyage of incremental decisions and wise investments. But when done intentionally and wisely, it not only guarantees your financial serenity in the sunset years but breathes life into your longstanding dreams. With this information, we hope you are armed with all you need to begin shaping a secure tomorrow today. Because it's rightfully said, "The best time to plant a tree was 20 years ago. The second best time is now."

# Chapter 10. Insurance Intelligence: Protecting Wealth with Awareness

The art of managing wealth extends beyond merely multiplying it. True financial literacy includes the principles of value multiplication, preservation, and, moreover, protection. Insurance, often overlooked amidst the dazzle of investments, yields its quiet, steadfast shield, serving as an essential armor fortifying one's wealth kingdom.

This exploration into the intricate universe of insurance aims to initiate a mindful dialogue around its relevance, types, role in wealth protection, and the application of consciousness when treading these paths. It's about perceiving insurance not as a grudging mandate, but as a mindful investment, a watchful protector, and above all else, an enabler of financial peace.

## 10.1. Penny Wise, Pound Foolish: Why Insurance?

Insurance occupies an interesting space in the financial canvas, often surrounded by a cloud of misunderstanding. There's a common perception of insurance as an unnecessary expense until disaster strikes, revealing the cracks in this negligent outlook.

Imagine you've toiled through years, carving out a path of financial stability and prosperity. Suddenly, an unforeseen event sweeps across this path, threatening everything you've worked for. Here, insurance steps in as your safety net, sheltering and preventing your hard-earned wealth from a potentially disastrous fallout.

A proper comprehension of insurance's necessity calls for a

reframing of our attitude. When we view insurance not as an imposed expenditure but as a careful investment safeguarding our wealth, we begin interacting with it more mindfully.

## 10.2. The Shield's Spectrum: Types of Insurance

An understanding of the diverse kinds of insurance available is vital to decide which would best suit your unique financial scenario. Here are some main types of insurance policies:

- Life Insurance
- Health Insurance
- Property Insurance
- Motor Insurance
- Travel Insurance
- Liability Insurance

Each type of insurance offers a different shield to protect various facets of your wealth kingdom. These shields are not mutually exclusive; they can and should be used collectively to create a holistic fortification around your investment portfolio.

## 10.3. Building the Bastion: Role of Insurance in Wealth Protection

There are three key functions that insurance carries out in the sphere of wealth management: risk management, safeguarding assets, and facilitating financial goals.

Firstly, insurance acts as a potent tool for risk management. Life is replete with uncertainties. Whether it's a damaging storm affecting one's property or a critical medical situation throwing a spanner in financial plans, insurance policies bear the brunt of these unforeseeable blows, thus minimizing risk.

Secondly, insurance avails protection for one's assets. Our assets - homes, cars, investments - aren't invincible. They're subjected to multiple perils, both anticipated and unanticipated. Insurance ensures these tangible wealth manifestations aren't left vulnerable.

Finally, insurance assists in accomplishing financial goals. It supports liquidity management, aids the wealth multiplication mechanism, and provides financial support during untoward circumstances. Therefore, dreaming of an enduring prosperity journey without the strategic incorporation of insurance seems almost incongruous.

# 10.4. Awakening Insight: How to be Mindful in Insurance

As we approach insurance with a mindful lens, some key factors emerge that can significantly streamline this process.

Before plunging into a policy, it's essential to carry out a comprehensive analysis of your financial landscape, which includes your income sources, investment portfolio, total assets, liabilities, and your financial goals. This information assists in determining the level and type of coverage apt for you.

Consider the myriad types of insurance policies and understand each one's particular benefits. More than merely buying a policy, it's about fostering a long-term relationship with these protective shields.

Lastly, it's crucial to do a meticulous comparison among different insurance providers, factoring in aspects like claim settlement ratio, premiums, policy inclusions and exclusions, customer reviews, and the company's credibility.

# 10.5. Nurturing the Nurturer: Regular Policy Review

A key aspect of mindful insurance practice is continual policy review and updates. As life unfolds, our financial needs, conditions, and goals evolve - requiring our insurance policies to reflect these changes accurately. It's a dynamic process, not a dormant document.

If insurance is the sturdy anchor celebrating financial tranquility, then awareness becomes the guiding compass maneuvering through this intriguing realm. The mantra is simple: Protect with vigilance, and insure with awareness. This prudent blend of insurance intelligence and mindfulness can redefine the age-old dance between money and protection—bringing resonance to the symphony of sustainable wealth management.

# Chapter 11. Roadmap to Prosperity: Your Unique Wealth Journey

This path to prosperity is as unique as you are. It is not a cookie-cutter methodology, but rather an individualized approach to wealth creation that can deliver enormous personal and financial rewards. Let's set off on this exciting journey together, unveiling the pillars that bring about a prosperous life, charged with monetary abundance and contentment.

## 11.1. Define Your Financial Goals

Like charting a course on a map, defining your financial goals is the initial and paramount step of your wealth journey. Without clear goals, the path to prosperity can seem nebulous and difficult to navigate. Your financial goals may range from short-term objectives such as paying off student loans or saving for a vacation, to long-term aspirations such as purchasing a home, planning for retirement, or setting up a college fund for your children. Each goal should be SMART: Specific, Measurable, Achievable, Relevant, and Time-bound. This approach makes the path toward your financial dreams more tangible and manageable.

## 11.2. Understand Your Current Situation

Taking stock of your current financial situation is an integral step in moving toward your financial goals. It includes assessing your assets (things you own), liabilities (debts you owe), and your net worth (assets - liabilities). This deeper understanding works like a personal balance sheet, providing a snapshot of your fiscal health and serving as a reference point from which you can track your progress.

## 11.3. Develop a Personalized Strategy

With your goals identified and your current situation outlined, it's time to formulate your personalized wealth growth strategy. This may involve diversifying your income sources, optimizing your tax situation, investing wisely, and setting up an emergency fund. You may benefit from the expertise of financial advisors, though it's important to note that no one cares more about your money and your future than you do. Therefore, equip yourself with sufficient financial knowledge to confidently participate in these strategic decisions.

## 11.4. Implement Your Strategy

Taking action is where the proverbial rubber meets the road. This phase involves deploying your individualized strategy, whether that's altering your expenses, adopting a consistent investing habit, or restructuring your debts. It's beneficial to automate your savings and investments to guarantee consistent implementation. Remember, the journey to wealth is not necessarily about making monumental leaps but rather taking consistent, calculated steps towards your financial goals.

## 11.5. Regular Review of Your Plan

A plan is only as good as its execution, and regular reviews are essential to ensure that you are on track with your wealth creation strategy. Regular audits allow you to adjust your plan as life circumstances change, such as a new job, marriage, childbirth, or even a global pandemic. These review and adjustment phases ensure your plan remains relevant and effective in achieving your goals.

# 11.6. Persistence is Key

The journey to financial prosperity is rarely easy, requiring tenacity, resilience, and discipline. There will be setbacks, but keep in mind that your wealth journey is a marathon, not a sprint. Persistence will prove to be your most truthful ally in this journey.

# 11.7. Embrace Mindfulness

Lastly, integral to your wealth journey is the practice of mindfulness. This refers to being 'present' in your financial decisions and being engaged with your money in an intentional way. It means not just allowing your financial life to happen to you, but actively shaping and directing it towards your chosen goals.

This journey toward prosperity also emphasizes the importance of financial serenity - the peace that comes from having control over your fiscal situation. It's not simply about accruing more wealth, but nurturing a healthier relationship with your money—one that enables you not only to meet your financial goals but also to lead a life full of contentment and joy, where wealth and happiness comfortably coexist.

There we have it - an idiosyncratic blueprint for your individual wealth journey. Each of these signposts leads the way to financial prosperity. Remember, this journey is no sprint but a marathon, your marathon. Take the step, engage in the dance, and empower yourself to flourish on this tailor-made path to sustainable wealth creation. It's more than a journey; it's your journey, marked by financial peace and prosperity. It's a golden opportunity to establish a legacy of wealth - not just for you - but for generations to come.